From Kansas to Cannibals:
The Story of Osa Johnson

From Kansas to Cannibals:
The Story of Osa Johnson

by

Suzanne Middendorf Arruda

Avisson Press, Inc.
Greensboro

TITLE VI

First edition
Printed in the United States of America
ISBN 1-888105-50-X

Library of Congress Cataloging-in-Publication Data

Arruda, Suzanne Middendorf, 1954-
    From Kansas to cannibals: the story of Osa Johnson / by Suzanne Middendorf Arruda.-- 1st ed.
    p. cm. -- (Avisson young adult series)
    Includes bibliographical references and index.
    Summary: A biography of the female explorer Osa Johnson who, with her husband Martin, made films about the Solomon Islands and Africa between the years 1920 and 1940.
    ISBN 1-888105-50-X (pbk.)
    1. Johnson, Osa, 1894-1953--Juvenile literature. 2. Johnson, Martin, 1884-1937--Juvenile literature. 3. Women photographers--United States--Biography--Juvenile literature. 4. Women cinematographers--United States--Biography--Juvenile literature. 5. Women explorers--United States--Biography--Juvenile literature. [1. Johnson, Osa, 1894-1953. 2. Johnson, Martin, [1884-1937. 3. Photographers. 4. Cinematographers. 5. Explorers. 6. Women--Biography.] I. Title. II. Series.

TR140.J63 A85 2001
910'.92--dc21
[B]
                                                     2001034829

Photos appearing in this book are courtesy of the Martin and Osa Johnson Safari Museum in Chanute, Kansas.

Note to the reader

When I read about someone's life, I want to know if everything I read was really true. Everything in this book happened. Nothing has been made up. Even the words in quotes are taken directly from Osa Johnson's books. Those books are listed at the end if you would like to read them. If your library doesn't have it, they might be able to get one on loan. Ask the librarian.

Suzanne M. Arruda

Acknowledgements

I would like to thank my husband, Joe, and my sons Michael and James for their help and support, and my friend Leatha Bolinger for teaching me how to edit my own work. I also want to thank Mr. Conrad Froehlich and Mrs. Barbara Henshall of the Martin and Osa Johnson Safari Museum for their help with research and with pictures.

This book is dedicated to all explorers, even if you are only exploring your own town. Be adventuresome!

Table of Contents

Chapter 1
Chanute, Kansas

Seven-year-old Osa begged her father, William Leighty, for ten cents. In the summer of 1901 ten cents was a small fortune, especially when Mr. Leighty only earned a dollar and twenty-five cents a day as a Santa Fe Railroad brakeman. But Osa was serious. This was important. She insisted she would even give up her Christmas present that year for the dime. The idea shocked Osa's grandmother. When she was seven, she'd never even seen a dime much less a present, and now her granddaughter was demanding enough money to buy a pound of round steak or two yards of calico.

Osa hurriedly explained that a traveling photographer was in town. Her good friend, Babe Halloran, took her baby brother to be photographed, and Osa felt strongly that she should take her own little three-year-old brother, Vaughn. It must be today. The pho-

Osa Leighty as a little girl in Chanute, Kansas

tographer lived and went to school in Independence, Kansas, and he was leaving tomorrow to go back to school.

Mr. Leighty was amused but uncertain. Ten cents sounded very pricey for a young high school photographer. Osa assured him the pictures were quality portraits. The ten cents bought a dozen pictures, not just one, and they were "the cutest you ever saw." She got the dime.

Little Vaughn Leighty had other ideas. He resented being pulled a dozen blocks through the hot streets of Chanute, Kansas in uncomfortable dress clothes and heavy, copper-toed shoes. He dragged his heavy shoes through piles of dust. He cried, and the dust streaked in ripples down his cheeks. They climbed the dark stairs to the upper floor of the Williams' Opera House.

Vaughn was still howling.

The tall, thin photographer peered out from under a black, cloth hood and ordered them to sit down and be quiet. They sat down on a box while the young man finished photographing a smiling baby girl. Osa licked her handkerchief and tried to clean the smudges from Vaughn's face. She smoothed his hair and tidied his shirt. If she expected the photographer to help her, she was mistaken. Instead, he rudely pulled off Vaughn's embroidered white collar and deliberately messed up his hair. Vaughn was delighted. He grinned. The result was a picture of a happy but messy-looking little toddler. Osa was furious.

The photographer took Osa's dime and told her to come back in the afternoon for the pictures instead of tomorrow. He was leaving early in the morning. Many years later Osa would meet that photographer again. He would sit in her living room and look at the family album. He would recognize the picture he took of Vaughn and laugh. He, Martin Johnson, would marry Osa and take her places no white woman had gone before. That was not the life Osa grew up to expect.

Osa's childhood was not unusual. She was born March 14, 1894 in Chanute, Kansas. Her mother, Ruby Isabelle (Belle) Leighty and pioneer grandmother, Nancy Ann Taylor, taught her how to cook, clean, and sew. They stressed the importance of home-making for a happy, healthy family. Her father taught her to fish in the Neosho River. In the winter they hunted for rabbits, and in the summer she helped him tend his garden. She loved doing domestic jobs and longed for a little house of her own to raise children with her husband. She and her high school friend, Gail Perigo, even made a pact to get married on the same day and live next door to each other.

Osa learned something else from the women in her family. She learned that a woman could be different from other women and still be a good wife and mother. Osa's mother, Belle, was the best card player in the county, and Belle got married when she was only fifteen. Osa grew up on stories of pioneer bravery from her grandmother who overcame many difficulties on the frontier. But the real break from tradition came from Osa's aunt Minnie who rode a pony bareback in a circus and smoked cigars.

So Osa began to see that life was full of different opportunities and adventures. She loved singing and performing in school assemblies as much as she loved fishing, cooking, and gardening. To Osa there was no conflict here, and her own dreams grew from these enjoyments. In her dreams she would grow up, be a great actress, and live in a lovely little home where she cooked, cleaned, and took care of her husband and children. What she didn't know was that the homes and gardens would be temporary, far-away places, and that pet gibbons, elephants, and cheetahs would replace the children. Osa would appear as a star in many movies, but her co-stars would be lions, rhinos, and head-hunters.

Chapter 2

"We're Going Around the World"

Osa and Captain Trask were the only two people not seasick on the Sonoma. Osa came on deck looking for breakfast when a huge wave broke next to her and hurled her to the other side of the ship. Captain Trask was furious. He demanded to know why she wasn't sick below "like other decent folk."

"I don't want to be sick," Osa shouted back. "I'm starved."

The Captain grinned and invited her to dine with him. He was taking a liking to the little Mrs. Johnson. At first he hadn't approved of Martin's young wife. She looked too soft and young. She was young. Sixteen-year-old Osa Leighty eloped with Martin Johnson after a whirlwind courtship, and for seven years they toured the United States giving travel shows. Now she was sailing to the South Seas with Martin to film cannibal headhunters. Osa's visions of being an actress and having a home near her family were washed overboard with the waves crashing on the freighter. How could this have happened?

Petite, brown-eyed Osa saw the tall, handsome young explorer when he came to Chanute, Kansas in November, 1909. Martin traveled to small towns talking about his adventures in the South Seas with author Jack London aboard a ship called the *Snark*. Osa didn't really go to hear Martin speak. She went to hear her best friend, Gail Perigo, sing at the Chanute theater where Martin was giving his lecture. In fact, Osa walked out on Martin's talk because she felt the pictures of the cannibals were horrid. She didn't recognize the young photographer who made Vaughn look like an orphan.

Martin asked Gail to sing at the *Snark No. 2*, his theater in Independence, Kansas. Gail was happy to oblige since her former sweetheart, Dick Hamilton, was the theater operator. Gail quit school, moved to Independence, and married Dick on the stage of the theater. Osa was angry and blamed everything on Martin. She always planned on having a double

Newly-weds Martin and Osa Johnson

wedding with Gail in Chanute and living side by side as friends forever.

Gail invited Osa to visit her in Independence, Kansas. Osa's mother and grandmother allowed Osa to visit since Gail was a married woman and a proper chaperone, but they reminded Osa to only speak to men in uniform. Osa took a train to Independence and tried to find Gail's apartment above the *Snark No. 2* theater. When she realized she was at the *Snark No. 1*, she asked directions from the ticket man and realized too late that it was Mr. Johnson. He offered to take her down the street to the other theater, but Osa walked off. Martin followed her to Gail's apartment where Gail formally introduced Osa to Martin. Osa decided not to be impressed, but she couldn't help noticing Martin's nice, wide-set, gray-green eyes.

Gail's husband, Dick, said Gail saved a piece of wedding cake for Osa to sleep on. Osa saw Martin stare at her when Dick mentioned the wedding cake. She noticed she was "shivering very pleasantly."

Martin also managed to drop by the

Hamilton's apartment the next time Osa visited Gail. Gail seemed to have matchmaking in mind, and Martin was happy to go along with the idea. Martin hired an automobile and drove them all to Coffeyville, Kansas. It was Osa's first car ride, and she was impressed with Martin's driving skill. She later wrote " I began to see that he was quite a remarkable man, though, of course, I must never let him see I thought anything one way or the other. That would be bold."

The two couples went to a dance pavilion, but Martin didn't ask Osa to dance. She told him his cannibal pictures were horrid. They next went to a skating rink, but Martin didn't skate. Wherever they went, people recognized Martin. Osa was angry. She felt Martin was ignoring her.

"I'll show him he isn't the only person around that can do things," she thought.

A roller skating chariot race was announced, and Osa filled in for another girl as the driver of two boys harnessed together. Osa wrapped the leather reins around her wrists so they wouldn't slip, and she skated as well as she knew how. Martin gripped the side of his seat and stared as Osa raced by. The boys she 'drove' wore new skates with ball bearings, and they skated on a new, smooth floor. That meant speed, and Osa just missed a turn. She flew over the fence and into the seats near the rink.

"Are you hurt bad?" asked Martin when he reached her.

"Of course not," she answered shortly.

Osa, Martin, Gail, and Dick left the rink. Martin drove, but Osa refused to sit with him in the front seat. When Martin mentioned that she would be black and blue, Osa threw a lap blanket over his head. Luckily, Dick grabbed the wheel in time to keep them out of a ditch. They rode back to Gail and Dick's apartment in silence, and Osa decided to go home to Chanute that night. Osa knew she was in love. Why else would she foolishly show off like that? And what else would cause her to ache so much inside when she thought she'd never see Martin again?

Martin knew he wanted Osa. The spunky little lady with hair the color of golden taffy impressed him. She was everything he wanted in a girl. Martin admired Jack London's wife, Charmian, who traveled with Jack to the South Seas. She could shoot and was clever and brave, and Osa showed the same spirit.

Martin wrote to Osa saying he would visit that coming Sunday. He wanted to meet her family. Osa spent the day cooking, baking, and re-doing her hair. Martin came, but it was so late that Osa had gone to bed disappointed and had to get up again. The entire family sat in the living room and tried to make polite conversation. Osa's brother Vaughn ate the box of chocolates that Martin brought.

Martin came another Sunday with a larger box of chocolates. Everyone sat in the living room and stared at each other, so Belle brought out the family photo album to help the conversation. Martin recognized the picture of Vaughn and laughed. It was not a very good beginning for a relationship.

Then Martin called from Independence and asked Osa to sing in his theater. Gail was sick with a sore throat. Osa's mother and grandmother didn't approve. She needed to be chaperoned. Martin put his own parents on the phone. They promised to take care of Osa, so Osa went to Independence.

Osa sang as well as she could that May 15th in 1910. It wasn't easy, because Martin gave her the wrong sheet music. Osa knew the melody played by the piano player, so she made up words as she went. She rhymed "above" with "love" and "spoon" with "June." She hit and held a high note at the end. The audience loved it. Did Martin? He said he was tone deaf, and music was just noise to him. Osa wondered what there was about this young man that made her feel the way she did and also made her angry all the time. But the adventure strengthened Osa's decision to become an actress.

Osa's father now worked as a railroad engineer so he wasn't home when Osa got the call to go to Independence. He came home, found Osa gone, and called the Johnsons to tell Osa to come home. Martin took Osa to the station. The train wasn't due for two hours, but Osa had insisted on leaving right away. Martin sat next to her.

"Will you marry me?" he asked.

"Yes," answered Osa, when she managed to get words out.

"Right away, I mean?"

"Yes."

"Tonight?"

"Yes."

They were married by nine o'clock that night in Gail's apartment, then they went on the train to Kansas City, Missouri to get married again in another state. Martin feared that Mr. Leighty would annul the marriage since Osa was so young. That began the lifelong partnership of Osa and Martin, a partnership that led Osa to places no other "civilized" woman had traveled before.

The couple spent seven years traveling around the rural west to mining towns in Colorado and Canada. They needed money for exploring. Martin lectured with his lantern slide show and Osa sang "Hawaiian songs." The miners loved hearing anything about Jack London and flocked to hear the couple.

But the ten cent admission price made it difficult to save money for a movie camera.

Osa Johnson in her "Hawaiian " costume.

Sometimes they slept in railroad stations because all the camp shacks were for "men only." Osa was no prima donna demanding luxuries. She knew the importance of a movie camera for their future and intended to sacrifice for it. Already she showed the determination that eventually carried the Johnsons through many rough adventures.

Their popularity on the lecture circuit convinced friends, family, and some businessmen to invest in them. Suddenly they had $4000 and made plans to head for the South Seas to film genuine cannibals and head-hunters.

Osa threw herself into planning for the trip. They both needed denim pants and durable, "huck" shirts. She worried about snakes, and decided she'd need boots. Osa thought she should cut her long, heavy hair, but Martin didn't like the idea. Just before they left, Osa met the famous Jack London and his explorer-wife, Charmian. They concluded Osa was just what Martin needed. Martin was so happy he dubbed Osa "Snarkette." Osa was going to become an official explorer.

Now, on board the *Sonoma*, she felt her excitement building. Plans became reality. It was just as she told all her friends, "We're going around the world!"

Chapter 3
So Frightful as to be Magnificent

All the missionaries and traders advised Osa to stay behind in Tulagi with the Governor of the Solomon Islands. She would be safe there. Even Martin promised Mrs. Leighty that Osa would stay with missionaries. They didn't know Osa. She had no intention of being left behind, not after enduring a voyage aboard a small steamship complete with cockroaches. She saw herself as Martin's partner and this as her delayed honeymoon trip. She also knew Charmian London wouldn't let Jack leave her behind, and Osa wanted to live up to Charmian's image. The only person who understood was Osa's grandmother, Nancy Taylor. She knew what it was like to be a pioneer in a wild territory. She felt a little adventure was good for people.

Osa and Martin arrived in the South Seas in 1917 with one hand-cranked motion-picture camera, two still cameras, photographic plates, two revolvers, Jack London's Marlin rifle, a few thousand feet of motion-picture film, a tin of baking powder, and a small sack of flour.

They went into Malaita's interior hills which teemed with stinging ants, biting spiders, poisonous plants and snakes, and butterflies the size of pigeons. Osa was an instant curiosity in the villages. None of the natives had ever seen a white woman before. She became Martin's ambassador, shaking hands with natives infected with sores and ringworm, holding their babies, and posing alongside warriors armed with spears. Osa was happy to pose with islanders for the films. It was almost like being an actress.

Osa worked hard to learn *Beche-de-mer*, the trade language of the islands. She practiced with Martin, traders, and with their hired help. *Beche-de-mer*, named for the edible sea slugs that the natives sold to traders, mixed native words with English. Once they were stopped by a native holding the hand of a little girl who was covered in a scaly ringworm disease called buckwa. The disease made her unfit for marriage. He asked them in *Beche-de-mer* if they wanted to buy her to eat.

"You wanta buyum this one fellah? Man belong him; him good kai kai (food); good fellah too much. Him sellum this one fellah Mary belong you."

A horrified Osa gave the man forty sticks of tobacco for the girl. If she didn't, she knew he would sell her to a native, and the girl would be eaten. They left the girl at a missionary station. It was proof that cannibalism was still practiced on these islands.

Wherever they went in the Solomons, Osa practiced the primary "don'ts" taught to her by a trader. Don't make advances first. Smile, but don't make the natives think you are making fun of them. Don't treat the natives with disrespect. Don't turn your back on the natives or let them surround you. Don't go into a hut unless it is safe. Don't pick flowers, until you know which are taboo and which are not. Don't touch spears and arrows; they might be poisoned. Many trails were taboo to women, so don't walk off alone. And don't go anywhere unarmed.

Osa didn't intend to simply tag along. She felt responsible for Martin's health and learned as much first aid as the doctor in Tulagi could teach her. She learned to dress wounds, splint broken bones, treat for reactions to poisonous plants and insects, and to protect them both from infection. Once, when Martin's eyes were swollen shut from hornet stings, Osa bathed his face with ammonia to reduce the swelling and relieve the pain. Later, Martin endured a malaria attack with a fever of over one hundred and four degrees. Osa gave him quinine and bathed his forehead to reduce the fever. But the doctor cautioned her not to play doctor with the islanders. If they died, others would kill her even if it wasn'ther fault.

Osa paid a lot of attention to the women and children and sometimes trilled like a canary to amuse them and gain their confidence. When the wives were happy, the village chief was usually happy and cooperative. Then Martin could take pictures and movies. They toured Guadalcanal, Savo, and New Georgia where Osa paddled about the lagoons with the native children and fished, a favorite activity since childhood in Kansas. She watched the island women cook fish with hot stones and always took an interest in their everyday lives.

Osa learned languages quickly. As her *Beche-de-mer* improved, so did her skill at bartering, providing Martin and herself with a wider variety of foods than the canned goods they brought with them. She knew their survival depended on staying healthy and alert. Osa even learned to grow her own yeast for bread by mixing raisins, flour, sugar, lime juice, and water and letting it ferment.

The Johnsons filmed splendid native dances on San Cristobal. On the island of Ulawa they photographed beautifully constructed native canoes crafted of wooden planks sewn together with vine, caulked with beeswax, and decorated with inlaid mother of pearl. Martin went into the "head huts," taboo to Osa and other women, to photograph the collections of heads and skulls. They saw fierce-looking native warriors with decorations of human shinbone in their noses. But the Johnsons were disappointed.

Government ministers and missionaries

changed the Solomon Islands. Everyone was "too civilized," and the Johnsons refused to stage primitive scenes. They wanted genuine wild tribes untouched by civilization. Martin and Osa needed to find something worth filming soon because expenses were great. They would soon be out of money. Their hope was in the New Hebrides.

These islands had been in conflict between the British and the French for so long that no one ever managed to take control except to send gun boats and fire on the islands after uprisings. The warfare started because traders raided villages and brutally kidnapped natives to work on ships or plantations. The only white people these natives met were cruel. One year before the Johnsons arrived, some natives killed a plantation family and ate them. When soldiers landed to punish the islanders, the natives led the soldiers into the dense jungle and killed them, too. It would be dangerous for Martin and Osa to land.

They sailed to the New Hebrides and first landed on the tiny island of Vao where a Catholic priest took care of lepers and elderly natives. Martin borrowed an unused whale boat to sail to the island of Malekula where the fierce "Big Nambas" tribe of head-hunters lived. He wanted Osa to stay behind with Father Prin.

"If you go, I'm going with you, Martin Johnson," she said angrily. "That's what I came for and that's how it's going to be — the whole way. The whole way!" she repeated.

An earthquake and an underwater eruption interrupted their first landing. The sea boiled around them, cooked fish floated to the surface, and hungry sharks preyed on the fish. The nearby villagers who saw the boat might assume the Johnsons caused the earthquake and kill them. Martin and Osa sailed farther south before landing on Malekula with some of Father Prin's interpreters.

Several Big Nambas men came out of the forest to meet them. They all wore wide belts of bark around their waists with plant fibers (nambas) hanging down the front. The Big Nambas men told the Johnsons their chief, Nagapate, (also known as Nihapat) saw their boat and wanted to meet them. Again Martin wanted to leave Osa behind, but she gathered up some calico and tobacco and followed. They slid and stumbled up a dark, treacherous trail wet with hidden streams, climbing at least a thousand feet up to the village. Natives moved in behind them. They broke one of the "don'ts" and let themselves get surrounded.

Suddenly before them "stood a figure so frightful as to be magnificent." Nagapate's face was framed in a thick black beard, and a bone pierced the cartilage of his nose. "His eyes showed intelligence, strong will, and cunning." Martin started filming. Osa acted as ambassador again and presented the chief with calico and tobacco. It was clear, however, that the powerful chief was interested in Osa when he reached out and grabbed her arm.

He rubbed her skin, removed her hat and examined her yellow hair. Then he began to study the back of her neck. Martin kept filming, and Osa stifled her terror and forced a smile. Was Nagapate only curious or did he plan to kill them? Osa did not know. She put some tobacco in Nagapate's hands but he dropped it immediately. Martin took the camera off the tripod and told Osa to go down the trail with the carriers. Nagapate took Osa's hand and shook it. Osa laughed in relief and returned the hand shake, but when she tried to pull away, he gripped her hand in his fist and began to pinch and prod her arm. Then suddenly, Nagapate released her.

The Johnsons dashed for the trail. Native ritual drums called boo boos began beating, and warriors grabbed Osa from behind. She screamed and saw that Martin was also caught, and a native was raking his back with a thornbush. Osa screamed again. The natives stopped. The boo boos stopped. Everyone was staring at the British patrol boat steaming into the bay.

Martin wriggled free and shouted at Nagapate, "Man-o'-war, Man-o'-war, Man-o'-war!"

Nagapate released them and withdrew into the bush. Martin and Osa walked slowly down the trail until they were out of sight. Then they raced to the beach, falling and scrambling down the sheer, slippery slopes. Vines and branches slapped their faces. For a while they were lost in the dense green forest, and the sound of beating boo boos told them Nagapate would be in pursuit soon. They found the beach and their crew dragged them onto the whaleboat as Nagapate's men emerged from the brush.

The trip was a success. Despite the rains and mud, the film was saved. The Johnsons had a tremendous movie they called *Cannibal Land,* but they were still not satisfied. They had pictures of skull huts and fierce looking natives including Nagapate himself. They did not have any pictures of an actual cannibal feast.

Two years later, in 1919, Martin and Osa returned to New Hebrides and to Malekula Island. Nagapate watched their boat from the beach and asked to come aboard. On the schooner, they showed Nagapate a full length poster of him. Then Martin handed Osa her ukelele, planted a kiss on her cheek, and asked Osa to sing. Osa played and sang "Aloha." To their surprise, Nagapate swayed his head with the rhythm and sang a chant of his own in perfect time to the music. They rowed him back to shore loaded with gifts of tobacco, knives, calico, and a top hat.

The next morning, many members of the Big Nambas tribe were on the beach yelling and waving their arms. Martin and the captain of the schooner went ashore, then quickly came back for Osa. Nagapate had sent presents of yams, coconuts, and wild fruit for her; not for them.

The Johnsons decided to show Nagapate and his men the movie Cannibal Land. They set a screen and projector on the beach, and Osa sang to keep the natives till nightfall. The hand cranked generator wouldn't work at first, but suddenly the lights came on, and the natives turned their backs to the strange, bright screen. Osa boldly took Nagapate by the arm in a queenly manner, sat on the ground facing the screen, and indicated that she expected him to do the same.

Nagapate sat. The natives were struck dumb when Osa's face appeared on the screen. Martin wanted to film the natives' reactions when they saw themselves on the screen so he set up flares just after Nagapate's own face appeared on the screen.

The islanders were confused. They chanted

Osa and Nagapate, chief of the Big Nambas headhunters.

"Nagapate, Nagapate" as they recognized their chief, but the hiss and glare of the flares frightened them. Perhaps it reminded them of the gun boats. They ran for the brush. Osa calmly touched Nagapate's arm and smiled reassuringly. Nagapate was an intelligent diplomat. He would not show fear in front of his men. He sat back down and told his men to do the same. Martin started the film reel over again.

Most of the islanders were in the film made two years before, and they called out their names and howled with laughter when they recognized each other on the screen. The noise hushed when a man who died a year before appeared on the screen. The Big Nambas immediately became respectful to the Johnsons, especially to Osa. Just before the Johnsons returned to the schooner, Nagapate invited them to visit the village.

Once again Osa and Martin visited the village of the Big Nambas. They stayed for six days, and Osa tried very hard to make friends with the shy women and children. Nagapate kept presenting Osa with gifts of fruit. He acted like he was courting her, so Osa and Martin decided it was time to leave. Nagapate gave them a personal escort back to their schooner.

The Johnsons returned to Vao and spent several days sealing their motion picture cans and developing the still photos when a trader named Powler anchored in the bay. He was looking for Martin and offered to take the Johnsons to the island of Espiritu Santo. Powler believed they would find interesting activities there. They did.

After walking for three hours into the interior, they heard the rhythmic beating of boo boos and pushed towards the sound. Through the grass they saw a dozen natives dancing around a fire. The smell of roasting meat filled the air as Martin and Osa crept forward. Some natives sat down to eat. Meat hung from a spit above the fire, and a head was on the fire. Here was something worth filming. Martin and Osa actually captured a ritual head drying ceremony on film, and Osa had material for her own book, *Bride in the Solomons*.

Chapter 4
It's Paradise

It will be no trip for a woman," said Mr. Blayney Percival, the British East Africa game warden, when he warned the Johnsons of the dangers ahead.

Osa wanted to explode. "Oh! No trip for a woman! That again!"

Mr. Percival wanted Martin and Osa to go on a long safari in 1921 to Mount Marsabit in northern Kenya. A virtually unexplored lake teeming with wildlife capped the mountain. It sat high in an extinct volcanic crater shielded by thick forest, and a rugged, rocky desert surrounded the mountain. The lake was a secluded sanctuary for wildlife, a perfect place to do the job they came to Africa to do; make a film record of African wildlife before the animals were gone.

Still, Mr. Percival was right about the danger. He took Osa to the Nairobi cemetery.

"If you're going to know Africa," he said, "this is a good place to begin."

Osa counted nine tombstones carved with the short message "Killed by a lion." She saw other headstones that described death from buffalo, rhino, leopards, or just accidental shootings. The dangers in Africa were different from the ones Osa knew in the Solomons.

Both Osa and Martin had a lot to learn before attempting the trip. Learning Swahili was the easy part, especially for Osa who had a gift for languages. How to go on safari was the hard part. They began by making several practice safaris close to Nairobi. At first, Martin and Osa didn't have much luck filming wildlife. They weren't used to filming in such intense sunlight, and the animals were either too far away or ran from them. They tried to get close to some buffalo in a ravine, but Osa and Martin ran up the sides when they thought the animals were about to charge. Their African staff were ashamed to be hired by two people who ran from danger. To make matters worse, explorers on safari supplied meat for their men, but Osa kept missing the animals. They needed to hire a professional hunter to shoot food for them.

While Martin practiced filming animals, Osa improved her shooting skills. She picked out an impala in a herd and brought it down with one shot. Soon after she brought down two charging buffalo. That won their staff over completely. From then on Osa was known in Africa as "Memsahib Kidogo" or Little Missus. They were ready for the big safari.

In 1921, the Johnsons set off with Martin's father, John Johnson, to find the hidden lake. Tents, ammunition, cameras, film, chemical developers, food, and clothing were all put into sixty-pound loads. They left for the Northern Frontier with four ox carts, a truck, and two cars, circling Mount Kenya on the hairpin turns and rugged inclines. Osa drove within inches of waterfalls which plunged into deep precipices. She coasted down steep grades where the load pushed her "almost out of control," and crossed "narrow, flimsy bridges that seemed to sag under us." It took one day to travel thirty-four miles.

Those roads were nothing compared to the

desert ahead. At Isiolo, the carts could go no farther. Neither could Martin's father. He and the ox carts turned back at a trading post near Isiolo, and 100 porters carried the supplies instead.

The march northward was a grueling nightmare. They walked at night to avoid the intense heat, but dried lava beds still sliced into their sandals, shoes, and feet. Water was scarce since the Guaso Nyiro River was the only permanent river in that part of Kenya. Between it and Mount Marsabit lay nothing but the wilderness of the Kaisoot desert, a vast wasteland that resembled a great, moon-like sea of hot sand and rock. Osa used her medical skills to repair everyone's damaged feet. Finally they arrived at the Marsabit government post at the base of the Marsabit Plateau. Above them somewhere in the mountain forest was the lake, but where? They needed a guide.

What happened next was like something out of a story. An aged native named Boculy lived at the Marsabit government post. He was nearly blind, and his jaw was crooked from a poorly healed injury, yet he possessed a "curious dignity." Boculy was an expert tracker known as the "little half-brother of the elephants." He sometimes worked as a tracker for the Kings African Rifles at the post when he wasn't in trouble for poaching. Boculy first pretended he didn't understand when Osa and Martin asked him about the lake. He seemed to be trying to decide whether or not to trust them. Boculy disappeared into the forest for five days, then returned like a ghost one evening.

"Tembo, mbwana, tembo mingi sana."
"Elephants, master, very many elephants."

Boculy took them up through the ancient Marsabit forest for several days along the elephant trails. They climbed on trails that wound through African olive trees heavily draped with bearded moss. They passed spectacular ravines where lions, leopards, and buffalo lived. Without warning, they broke through the trees to a cliff and overlooked a beautiful, spoon-shaped lake teeming with wildlife. Hardened lava formed a beach nearly 100-feet wide, and beyond the beach sloped the steep, forested banks. Huge, blue watlilies grew thickly in the shallow edges of the turquoise-

Osa and Boculy tracking elephants.

colored lake. Long-necked egrets and cranes dipped their heads gracefully in the water. An uncountable number of wild animals including elephants stood drinking in the lake.

"It's paradise, Martin!" said Osa, and Crater Lake got its new name of Lake Paradise.

Even though the crater lake had been visited before, very few people knew its actual location. Osa and Martin wanted it to stay a hidden reserve, so they decided to keep the location a secret. They spent three months at the lake filming elephants and other wildlife. The elephants at the Lake had little fear of the Johnsons , so Martin and Osa could get very close. Together with Boculy, they traveled over centuries-old elephant trails for their films.

Their movie *Trailing African Wild Animals* was a hit for many reasons. One of them was Osa. Audiences loved seeing tiny, five-foot two-inch Osa chasing an elephant or standing guard with her gun. The unstaged filming of wildlife also won support for their next African trip from the American Museum of Natural History and Mr. George Eastman, of Eastman-Kodak.

In 1924, they went back to the Lake with Blayney Percival for a four-year stay. Osa again drove one of the cars. It was loaded with film, camp tables, chairs, and two tents with poles. Waterproof containers sat strapped on the running boards, and the front fenders held bags of tarpaulins and ground cloths. The holster for Osa's gun sat on one side of the steering wheel, and her shotguns sat on the other side, both in easy reach.

"Is there any room for me to drive?" she asked Martin.

Osa wasn't going to travel in her car alone. Martin assigned two of their African staff, Suku and Toto, to ride with her. They carried Osa's pet Persian kittens on their laps. Finally Osa's pet gibbon, Kalowatt, jumped in and put her arms around Osa's neck. Kalowatt traveled everywhere with them, and Osa loved him.

Osa provided meat for the men on this trip, and she was often up fishing before Martin woke. There was no time to fish during the day. They had to keep moving to cross the Guaso Nyiro before the rains came and flooded the river. After long weeks of enduring ticks, bouncing over rocks, and pushing cars and wagons through rivers, they arrived at Lake Paradise. From below came the echoing booms of elephant herds pushing through the trees to the lake.

Osa felt she'd been dropped into the garden of Eden; a paradise. But just like The Garden of Eden, there were no other humans for company. It would be hard for Osa, who treasured friends and family. In her mind she imagined the house

Osa drives the truck on safari so that Martin can film.

of her dreams with children playing and neighbors chatting. Osa always longed for a real home, but she never expected it would be built at a hidden African lake. The idea overwhelmed her at first until she heard her grandmother's voice in her head saying, "What do you think our covered wagons found in Kansas, Sears Roebuck catalogs?"

Blayney Percival and Martin built the exterior of their home, and Osa took charge of finishing and furnishing the interior. She made a pink plaster from crushed, white lime rock and a rosy-pink rock. She built furniture from scrap logs, packing crates and rawhide. Antelope horns made hooks for hanging hats. More wood from packing crates turned into floor boards. Finally Osa planted a large garden with seeds from Kansas. Actually she planted two gardens. An old, mother elephant loved the sweet potatoes and frequently raided them. So Osa planted a second patch for the elephant and her babies.

But Osa's job was not to be a homemaker. Her job was to keep Martin alive, and preventing malaria spells with a healthy diet was only one of the ways she did this. Osa was now a "crack shot" providing meat for themselves and for the men who worked for them. She also stood by while Martin filmed charging animals, ready to deflect them at the last minute with shouts or shots if necessary. She had already proved her ability to do that several times.

On the Johnson's first trip to Lake Paradise, three elephants strolled past Osa and Martin's tent toward the lake. Martin grabbed his camera and began filming. He signaled Osa to move into the picture. Osa's only experience with elephants was seeing them in the circus. She didn't feel afraid until the elephants turned and faced her. Their trunks went up in alarm, and their ears stood straight out from their heads. Martin yelled for her to run, but Osa's feet felt like lead. She shivered in terror. Then suddenly, Osa started yelling at the elephants. She chased them. The elephants turned and ran.

Unfortunately, Osa was not always able to scare away the danger. Soon after they returned to Lake Paradise a charging elephant almost killed Martin. This time Martin was not behind the camera. He was trying to get an elephant's attention for some action while Osa cranked the camera. The elephant charged. Osa continued cranking until it was clear that Martin could not escape up a tree. She grabbed her rifle and fired. The elephant fell dead only six feet from Martin and knocked over the camera. Their staff was delighted with Osa. They carried her singing "Memsahib (mistress) has killed an elephant. Memsahib has killed an elephant. Little Memsahib is a big one."

That was not the only time Osa saved Martin's life in Africa. Filming wildlife meant getting close, and Martin was filming lions when one charged. Martin confidently kept cranking the camera, and Osa shot the lion within a few feet of her husband. But neither Osa nor Martin wanted to kill wildlife unless it was absolutely necessary. They were in Africa to make authentic films and didn't want the animals to become afraid of them. Unlike the other hunters in Africa who wanted trophies, Osa and Martin wanted to preserve wildlife on film and in reality.

To make their films they went on safari and

spent hours sitting in blinds up in trees or on the ground. They set up flash traps to photograph animals at night. Sudden storms drenched them, and ants bit them. Osa learned to sit through it all silently or the animals would be scared away. She became an expert tree climber to escape charging animals, and began taking flash pictures on her own.

Osa and Martin shared the beauty and danger of their home with only a handful of other people. Blayney Percival visited at the beginning of their stay, and Carl Akely from the American Museum of Natural History and George Eastman went on safari with them. Osa and Martin also entertained royalty. They traveled off the mountain to meet the Duke and Duchess of York, soon to become King George VI and Queen Elizabeth. Osa brought them a gift of fresh vegetables from her garden. They also met Prince Youssouf Kamal of Egypt. But most of these people did not stay at Lake Paradise. The Johnson's wanted it to be as free from hunting as possible.

Their *Four Years in Paradise,* as Osa titled her later book, ended all too quickly. Soon it was time to leave their beautiful home, the only permanent home that Osa had ever shared with Martin.

Chapter 5
Chant of Missonaries and Natives

The Lake Paradise camp was 'closed.' Misty mornings thick with the fragrance of wild jasmine and visions of rock-like silhouettes of elephants in the moonlight were part of the past. So was Carl Akely. Their good friend and explorer who first convinced them to go to Africa died on a safari in November, 1926, one month before the Johnsons closed up their Lake Paradise home. Osa grieved for the loss along with Martin. She lost a good friend and a home at the same time. There were many more changes waiting for Osa; changes involving family, friends, health, and their careers.

They decided to climb Mount Kenya in January, 1927 and picked up some staff in Nairobi and at the Chogoria Mission. January is summertime in Africa, but the top of Mount Kenya ignored that fact. The cold air at 12,000 feet froze the water in their wash basins. Osa always enjoyed good health in their travels, but

Mount Kenya changed that. The air and the water may have been cold, but Martin, Osa, and several of their men were not. They suffered from high fevers.

Martin sent the healthy men, including a Mr. Wilsheusen, down the mountain for Dr. Irwine, the mission doctor. He was gone, but Mr. Wilsheusen and the men took a truck up a timber track from the mission to get the Johnsons, actually hacking out a path for the truck. When the rescue party returned, Martin and the other men were already recovering, but Osa was unconscious and her lips were blue. She, Martin, and the others caught influenza, but Osa's case turned into a viral pneumonia followed by a bacterial pneumonia.

They took Osa to a grass hut at the mission and sent for an ice machine from Nairobi to bring down her fever. It took over a month for her to fully recover. Osa didn't remember much of the experience except "the strange beauty of a seemingly far-off bell and the soft chant of missionaries and natives."

She was still weak, and Martin felt that the best recovery for Osa was to go on safari to film lions. The idea worked. Soon Osa was able to walk and hold a gun again. But this trip didn't last long. Martin and Osa needed to go home to supervise the editing of their movies.

The Johnsons were celebrities when they arrived in New York City. This time, Osa was listed in the movie credits as a co-producer with Martin. Contracts for personal appearances paying hundreds of thousands of dollars were offered. Osa and Martin turned them down. All they wanted was enough money to continue doing what they loved to do; filming wildlife. But films were changing, too. People had discovered and now wanted movies with sound. The Johnson's would need to wait for some of the profits from their films *Simba* and *Safari* to buy new sound cameras.

George Eastman, who financed the Johnson's Paradise years, planned a safari to the headwaters of the Nile River. He invited Osa and Martin along while they waited. By December of 1927 they were once again leaving Osa's beloved family and heading to Africa. This two-month safari wasn't very difficult mainly because Mr. Eastman was over seventy years old. Osa loved him like a treasured uncle. He was a gourmet cook, and together they spent many happy hours cooking lemon pies and other treats on safari. He also took care of her when she came down with dysentery. Osa felt that would never see him again when they parted at the Sudan. She was right. Mr. Eastman died in March, 1932.

These deaths were very hard for Osa. She felt very strong attachments for friends and family and wrote to Charmian London, "I feel as if somebody had been smashing my heart with a hammer."

Osa and Martin's work would not stop with these partings. In fact, work was a good remedy for their loneliness. In 1929, the Johnsons began making the first sound picture of Africa. Adding sound wasn't the only change. They were now working with Fox Movie Studios instead of a museum.

They traveled to the Ituri Forest in the Congo to film the Mbuti Pygmies. Getting there was not easy. First they had to get to Lake Albert at the edge of the Belgian Congo. Next 150 cases of gasoline, hundreds of cases of food, boxes of ammunition, guns, tents, and other needed supplies were towed by a steamer thirty miles on a barge across the lake. Osa watched the barge sway and tip and worried that everything would be swallowed up by this rough inland lake. From Lake Albert they drove the steep, winding road to the government post of Irumu near the eastern edge of the forest, set up a temporary camp six miles from Irumu, and went into the forest in search of the shy Mbuti to ask them to assemble.

The Mbuti lived in the "darkest depths of the forest" where filming was impossible, so Osa and Martin built a village in the clearing by a stream and began coaxing the shy tribe to move there temporarily. Over 500 men, women, and children came from their forest homes. How would they move so many people? By car and truck.

The Mbuti wanted to cooperate but the cars terrified them. Osa smiled, pleaded, and made promises of calico and salt to get the women and children to ride in her car. The Johnsons filmed the Mbuti for several months, and Osa came to admire these small people. She wrote, "they showed neither hate, greed, vanity, envy, nor any of the other dominatingly unpleasant emotions of our so-called civilized world."

When the Mbuti returned to their nomadic lives in the forest, Osa and Martin attempted filming Mountain Gorillas in the Virunga Range. The popular idea about gorillas was of vicious, murderous brutes, but the Osa and Martin found the animals were shy. In fact, their shyness made gorillas hard to film. Osa was more involved in these movie productions. She gave directions to the sound technicians that came with them from Fox. She also took more flash pictures of animals at night.

The Johnson's Congo film crews included more American staff and fewer porters, which meant Osa didn't need to hunt as often. There was also less danger to Martin from elephant or buffalo attacks, so Osa had more spare time. She started writing and wrote a series of nine articles about baby animals for *Good Housekeeping* magazine. Osa hoped these stories would help children to not be afraid of animals. In 1930, these stories were put together in a book called *Jungle Babies*.

When people developed an new interest in flying, Martin and Osa decided to combine flying and movies. Osa's first solo flight in Chanute was hardly pretty. She took off fine. Landing was the problem. Osa reported "the ground came up with terrific speed and, hitting it, I bounced thirty feet in the air. My second and third tries at landing were exactly like the first. I'm not quite certain to this day how I managed finally to land the plane without having it bounce off the ground again, but land I did, and sat there for a minute marveling at my good luck."

They returned to Africa in 1931 with their own pilot licenses and two amphibious airplanes named *The Spirit of Africa* and *Osa's Ark*. These planes were built with bunks, a camp stove, storage cabinets, and a desk with a typewriter for Osa.

The Johnsons flew to Lake Rudolf and across the Serengeti. They went back to the Ituri Forest and flew several of the Mbuti pygmies in their planes. Osa was impressed by the Mbutis' ability to recognize landmarks from the air. Aerial safaris were different. They now

Top: Osa transporting Mbuti pygmies to film site in the Congo. Bottom: Camping under the wings of "Osa's Ark": sound crew Robert Moreno, Vern Carstens, Martin Johnson and Osa.

only needed thirteen men rather than the fifty or more that they needed before, but they could go farther and make more complete movies of wildlife.

Martin still wanted Osa to appear in the movies with the animals. The public loved to see the tiny lady stand her ground with an elephant or lion, and that made the movies more popular. They thought showing wildlife next to the airplane would also be interesting, so the Johnsons dragged a dead zebra up to *Osa's Ark* to attract lions. Martin set his camera nearby and Osa waited in the plane. When a pride of lions came by for the meat, Osa lifted the glass hatch and talked to the lions while Martin filmed the scene.

Most of the lions became used to the Johnsons. Often lions slept in the shade of the airplane, but one day a new male with a taffy-colored mane decided Osa looked more interesting than the zebra or the shade. The lion growled and charged the cockpit just as Osa pulled down the hatch.

Bang! The lion crashed against the glass at an angle. Martin kept on filming, but he was frightened for Osa. The glass was strong, but if the lion charged again head on, the glass might break. Osa was scared, too, but decided to teach the lion a lesson rather than shoot it. After all, they attracted him to the plane. She grabbed a carton of flour, opened the hatch, and flung the bag at the lion's head. The cardboard carton burst open and covered the lion's mane with flour. The puzzled lion trotted off to clean his coat first by licking, then by rolling in the grass. Martin recorded the entire adventure on film.

Osa believed in protecting the lions of the Serengeti. Once she found a mother lion and two small cubs five miles from water. The mother was thin from lack of food and water but wouldn't leave her babies. Osa took an empty five-gallon fuel can and cut the top off. She stood guard with the gun while Martin dug a hole for the can, then they filled it with water. Osa next shot a zebra which they carried to the can of water. The lioness first drank the water, then she dragged the kill back to her babies. The Johnsons refilled the water can and left the family in peace.

The aerial safari ended sooner than expected. Osa felt ill for many months, and Martin hired a nurse to travel with them to care for her. Finally Osa became sick enough to enter the Nairobi hospital, but she needed to go back to the United States for surgery. Martin fitted the *Osa's Ark* with a special bed, and they left Africa in 1934. In late August, Osa had a non-cancerous tumor removed in a New York hospital.

A terrible tragedy happened while Osa recovered from surgery. Her father was killed in a railroad accident four months before his retirement. His death was a horrible blow to Osa. Mr. Leighty had taught her to fish and shoot when she was a child. He gave her the passion for gardening and the outdoors, and it was Mr. Leighty that Osa took up as her first passenger when she learned to fly. One more beloved companion exited her life.

Osa always longed for a home near her parents. The long trips far away often made her very sad and lonely, yet she knew how important exploration and film-making was to

Martin. She also knew that film-making was changing. Their most recent feature films were more for entertainment, and neither sound footage nor the film industry was easy to work with. Osa worried about Martin, too. He had diabetes, and it was now necessary for him to take daily insulin injections. Osa didn't want to lose any more family.

Osa wanted them to take shorter trips and concentrate on making films for the lecture circuit. They now made a $1000 a week on a lecture tour with the Radio-Keith-Orpheum theaters to build up their finances. On this tour they showed their silent film *Wings Over Africa* while they waited for their feature film *Baboona* to be released by Fox.

Martin didn't like Osa's idea. He was now an independent-film producer and didn't want to be the "travelogue man" anymore. Their films had matured, too. The new movie showed the Johnson's own increasing respect for native cultures. Instead of accepting Osa's proposal, Martin decided to travel to Borneo for another feature film. Osa felt strongly that her place was with Martin, so in August of 1935, she left with Martin aboard a steamship for their last adventure.

Chapter 6
If They Fly, Walk, Wiggle or Crawl

Osa took her turn at the controls of their recently renamed plane, *The Spirit of Africa*, and became the first woman to fly over the China Sea as they headed towards Borneo. The Johnsons first tried filming in Borneo after their trip to the Solomon Islands, but it rained so much the film started to rot. This time they were more prepared. They even painted a huge eye on the nose of the plane. Bornean legend said this was the eye of a long dead god that guided travelers to their destination. Perhaps the Borneans would recognize the eye and trust the Johnsons.

In 1935, the Johnsons built a home camp on the Kinabatangan River. It included their personal house, buildings for their staff, a mess hall, a film laboratory, and an airplane hanger. Despite its size, "Johnsonville" wasn't built to last as long as their home in Lake Paradise. It didn't have a wall of thornbush around it for protection from elephants and lions and it also didn't have Osa's usual garden. She planted carrots, potatoes, peas, tomatoes, and lettuce, but the constant rain and the ants made gardening impossible in Borneo.

But Osa kept pets as always. Her pets were her children, and she loved them very much. In Borneo she shared her love with a pet honey bear named Honey Boy and a gibbon ape named Wah Wah. Osa and Martin also built a house-raft for traveling in comfort up the river to visit the native people.

Osa never encountered many snakes in Africa, but they seemed to be everywhere in Borneo. A deadly fer-de-lance crossed her path one night at their home camp. She returned with her gun, but it was gone. She saw a twenty-seven foot long python kill a wild boar in the jungle. Later she shot a twenty-eight foot long python at a rubber plantation. There were cobras and also "flying snakes" that leaped from tree to tree. When Martin asked her if they should stay she replied, "Of course. If the natives can outsmart these snakes, so can we. I don't care if they fly, walk, wiggle, or crawl."

Once again Osa was an ambassador with the native people. The women of the Dusun tribe were very shy, but with constant smiles, Osa was able to coax them to come out of their houses. They filmed many different tribes and native customs including dances and hunting with a blowgun and poison darts. These films became valuable records of vanishing cultures.

As in the past, Osa was examined carefully by any of the people who had never seen a white woman before. They rubbed her skin to see if the color stayed. They examined her teeth. Many of the native Borneans filed their teeth to a point and blackened them by chewing betel nuts. Her straight, white teeth were different. Osa learned long ago that most native people respected bravery and scorned fear. By standing still, smiling, and not screaming or running away when she was inspected, she gained the respect of the people.

Osa didn't always stay with Martin, especially when he was developing film. She led her own exploration into the jungles of Borneo. It was not an easy hike. Osa and her men hacked a path in the thick growth with sharp knives called "parangs." Sharp nanti dulu thorns tore her clothes and snagged her hair. Pale yellow leeches dropped off the leaves and fastened themselves to her exposed neck. Osa burned the leeches off with a lighted cigarette and pressed on into a gloomy swamp. She waded waist-deep through stagnant water and tripped over submerged roots and stumps.

The trip was worth the effort. About one mile from their camp, Osa found a beautiful hidden stream which "carved its silver path" between nipa palm trees and tall bamboo. Cedar and olive trees crowned the surrounding plateaus. The entire area was alive with hundreds of butterflies dancing in shades of blue, crimson, and pearly white like "engaging entertainers in attendance upon a host of maharajas." Instead of the maharajas, parakeets, hornbills, and other brightly colored birds watched alongside monkeys in the trees.

Osa ached all over, her head throbbed, she was covered in cuts and welts, but she was excited about her discovery. She knew Martin would be, too. The next day Martin came with her. They took canoes on the newly cleared

Osa and her favorite pet, Kalowatt.

path and explored the stream, filming the wildlife and the flowers.

Filming elephants in Borneo was different than in Africa. Cow herons followed herds in Africa. The Johnsons could tell if herds were feeding quietly, sleeping, or on the move by watching the herons. There were no cow herons in Borneo, so Osa and Martin had to watch the elephants' behavior more closely. If their ears went out and their heads rocked, the elephants were going to charge. Luckily, in Borneo there were always available trees to climb to escape. Martin said that Osa could climb like a scout.

Osa eventually wrote about both of the Borneo trips in one book, *Last Adventure*. In it she tells of canoeing on the rapids and of man-eating crocodiles. Some natives thought the crocodiles held the spirits of ancestors. They were revered and feared. Osa and some of their crew were canoeing against a strong current in rapid water when one of the men fell overboard and was swept downstream. Osa turned the canoe around and raced after him. Suddenly they saw the native dip below the water. Eight crocodiles from the opposite bank slid into the water after him. Osa raised her rifle and killed four crocodiles. She waited, but the lost man never resurfaced. Hours later, several crocodiles climbed onshore, and Osa killed them all. They cut open the animals and found part of a human leg in a crocodile's stomach.

Osa also described one of the most terrible adventures of her life in the village of the Tenggara tribe. The Tenggara had once been headhunters, but government rule had stopped most of that activity. Osa and Martin wanted to film their daily lives and customs and went to their village by canoe. They were alone deep in the Bornean jungle, cut off from civilization, when Martin suddenly had a very serious malaria attack and became delirious with fever. What was worse, the constant rains had soaked into their supplies and ruined almost all their quinine.

Osa was frantic. She ripped open box after box, looking for some of the desperately needed medicine. There was very little. Osa gave Martin what quinine they had and tried to keep him dry in their tent. As he sweat through one blanket, she wrapped him in another and

Osa and a Bornean native hunting with a blow pipe.

draped the wet blanket on boxes in the tent to dry, a nearly impossible task in the humid, stormy air. Outside the rain was coming down harder than ever. Lightning pierced the night in blinding flashes. Osa could not risk taking Martin back by canoe in the storm while the river was swollen and raging.

Then the Tenggara natives outside began to dance and chant in the terrible storm. They raised their hands to the trees and pounded their feet in the mud. Their wet bodies glistened in the flashes of lighting. Osa was grateful for the sound of other human voices. "I never dreamed that I would find comfort in the chant of a head hunter. But that is just what I did."

The eerie dancing and chanting continued until dawn; then it stopped. There was only the sound of the constant rain. Osa peeked out the tent and saw the natives going into the woods. She asked a native interpreter, Utar, what this meant. Why were they leaving them?

"Memsahib," Utar replied, " they are not leaving you. They are going into the forest to get some medicine for you to give to the sick one."

He told her that they could not gather

76

medicine at night or it would bring evil. During the night, the Tenggara danced and sang to ask their gods for permission to gather the medicine. Soon the medicine man returned with a mixture of herbs, berries, and shrubs crushed together. Osa tasted it and recognized the bitter taste of quinine. For several days she gave this medicine to Martin. His fever broke. He was weaker and thinner than before, but he was alive. The respect they gave to the Tenggara was repaid.

Afterword
"I am Simply Going Home"

Osa and Martin were back in New York cutting together their films from Borneo. They wanted a silent film, *Jungle Depths of Borneo*, to go with their lectures and a commercial film, *Borneo*, for the Fox Movie Company. The Johnsons always arranged their own lecture tour before, but the vaudeville circuit was disappearing. This time they hired Mr. Clark Getts to act as their agent for lecture bookings. By December, 1936, he'd arranged an $87,000 lecture and radio tour. The tour began in Salt Lake City, Utah talking to several thousand children in the tabernacle.

The lecture was a great success. Martin asked Osa to sit in the audience to help study the children's reaction. This was a treat for Osa. She loved children and never had any of her own. The children loved to see pictures of the animals. Girls "ohed" and "ahed" when Martin showed them pictures of orchids and told them

Osa had counted five hundred blooms on one branch. Boys and girls alike laughed at pictures of the proboscis monkey with its long nose.

The Johnsons left Utah on a commercial flight to California on Jan 12, 1937. The weather turned bad, and the plane iced up. It tossed and rolled, strayed three miles off course, and crashed in a mountainous area.

Osa and Martin were knocked unconscious. One man was killed instantly and thrown on top of Osa. Another passenger with a broken ankle crawled out of the wreckage and made his way to a sanitarium four miles away for help. The wreckage was not easy to reach. Hospital workers climbed to the plane with mules and a buckboard wagon. By the time help arrived the passengers were conscious and screaming.

Martin had multiple jaw fractures, broken legs, a broken nose, and a cerebral concussion. He was delirious. Osa tried to comfort him and wipe his forehead despite her own fractured right knee and back injuries. It took several hours to get passengers to the hospital in Los Angeles.

Martin's diabetes complicated his recovery.

Osa and her line of children's books and 'scientific' toys.

He went into a coma and died on January 13, 1937. Osa found out the next day. Jack London's widow, Charmian London, came to comfort her along with Osa's mother, Belle Leighty, and her brother, Vaughn.

In addition to her own injuries and the loss of her husband, Osa was in financial trouble now. The Johnsons never had much money. It was always tied up in movie production. Osa knew she must complete the lecture tour alone, both for financial reasons and as a tribute to Martin. To complicate matters, Martin's sister, Freda, was demanding more of the money from the lectures and film than Martin's will allowed. Osa's agent, Mr. Getts, helped Osa with these problems.

Osa courageously delivered her lectures from a wheelchair, but the wheelchair was not the only difficulty she had to overcome. Another was the nation's attitude towards women. In the 1930's it was improper for a woman alone to be lecturing. The theater managers finally agreed to let Osa speak but insisted on billing her as Mrs. Martin Johnson rather than as Osa Johnson. Mr. Getts worked hard to show the world Osa for herself. Many people didn't like this. They expected to see Osa as the faithful grieving widow. So when Osa eventually married Mr. Getts on April 29, 1940, it was in secret.

Mr. Getts helped Osa get a Hollywood contract with producer Darryl Zanuck. Mr. Zanuck wanted Osa to act as technical advisor for his movie, *Stanley and Livingstone*. In June, 1937 Osa sailed back to East Africa. For three months she gave valuable advice about everything from locations, hiring over a thousand Africans for the movie, filming wildlife, to running a camp efficiently. Osa proved herself to be a "master at bush craft."

Before she left for Africa, Osa wrote an editorial for *American Magazine*. In it she explained, "I have spent twenty of my last twenty-seven years in the jungles of Africa, Borneo, Australia, and the South Sea Islands, and now I am going back. Even to my friends my insistence upon returning, after a brief visit to civilization, may seem a bit dramatic. Some of them are grieved, imagining that I am deliberately seeking danger and perhaps death.

Others say they admire my courage. None of them understands. I am not returning to peril, privation, and hardship. I am simply going home."

Unfortunately for Osa, she could not stay in Africa. Lectures demanded her time. She wrote several books of her adventures: *I Married Adventure*, *Four Years in Paradise*, *Bride in the Solomons*, and *Last Adventure*. Osa also launched a line of clothing made from fabric called "Osafari." The clothing had wooden buttons that resembled African masks.

In February, 1941, Osa traveled to Winter Park, Florida to receive an honorary doctor of science degree from Rollins College. She also spoke at the Rollin's Annual Animated Magazine where nationally known writers and political figures spoke. Her own address was short, but rich with sincerity.

"With our old world dissolving before our eyes, most of us are desperately wondering, and trying to hold on to what remains of the good, the true, and the familiar....Opportunity is something that one has to make for himself, with laborious planning and doing and plenty of suffering...Nothing is impossible, if you want it badly enough, and if you have the imagination to dream and the energy to make your dreams come true."

Osa's family demanded more of her income in return for their past investments. Since family was always so important to her, everything seemed to be falling apart in her world despite her successes. Osa at once dreamed of stardom, adventure, home, and family. She struggled to achieve those in the best way she could no matter where she was. But the last years may have been harder on Osa than all the adventures combined. Money problems and family squabbles added a lot of stress. Osa Leighty Johnson died of a heart attack in her New York apartment at the age of fifty-eight on January 7, 1953. The courageous heart that carried her and Martin through so many difficulties finally failed her. She was buried in Chanute, Kansas next to Martin.

Today there is a museum in Chanute, Kansas dedicated to Martin and Osa Johnson. Visitors can see many of their photographs, their tremendous collection of masks, drums, and other cultural artifacts from their trips, and learn more about both of these dedicated explorers.

Bibliography

Imperato, Pascal and Eleanor, *They Married Adventure,* Rutger's University Press, New Jersey, 1992.

Johnson, Martin, *Over African Jungles: The Record of a Glorious Adventure Over the Big Game Country of Africa 60,000 Miles by Airplane,* Harcourt Brace and Co., N.Y., 1935.

Johnson, Osa, *Bride in the Solomons,* Boston, Houghton Mifflin Co., 1944.

Johnson, Osa, *Four Years in Paradise,* Philadelphia and New York, J. Lippincott Co., 1941.

Johnson, Osa, *I Married Adventure, The Lives and Adventures of Martin and Osa Johnson,* Philadelphia and New York, J. Lippincott Co., 1940.

Johnson, Osa, "Jungle," American Magazine,

Vol. 124, July 1937, p. 146.

Johnson, Osa, *Jungle Pets,* New York and London, G.P. Putnam's Sons, 1932.

Johnson, Osa, *Last Adventure: The Martin Johnsons in Borneo,* Edited by Pascal J. Imperato. New York: William Morrow and Co., 1966.

McCreedy, Frederick M., "An Analysis of Osa Johnson - Noted Female Explorer", Master's Thesis, Pittsburg State University, Pittsburg, KS 1998.

The Martin and Osa Johnson Safari Museum, 111 N. Lincoln Avenue, Chanute, Kansas.
www.safarimuseum.com

Index

From Kansas to Cannibals